Worlds Apart

RICHARD JACKSON

The University of Alabama Press
Tuscaloosa and London

Library of Congress Cataloging-in-Publication Data

Jackson, Richard, 1946–
  Worlds apart.

  (Alabama poetry series)
    I. Title. II. Series.
  PS3560.A242W6   1987   811'.54   86-30718
  ISBN 0-8173-0343-X
  ISBN 0-8173-0344-8 (pbk.)

British Library Cataloguing-in-Publication Data is available.

For my mother

Acknowledgments

I wish to thank the editors and publishers of the following journals in which some of these poems first appeared.

Antioch Review
  How Far the Light Travels
Concerning Poetry
  How We Make Sense of Things
Georgia Review
  The Promise of Light
Kenyon Review
  Unable to Refuse; What to Listen For
Long Pond Review
  Never Another Country
Louisville Review
  Wild Horses; The Green Heron; Whatever We See; Trying to
  Believe in Something; The Map
Maryland Review
  The Secret; From the Fort Payne, Alabama, Flea Market
New England Review and Bread Loaf Quarterly
  Wishbone
North American Review
  Why We See What We See
Ploughshares
  Worlds Apart; For the Nameless Man at the Nursing Home near
  the Shawsheen River
Poetry Northwest
  The Waterfall
Prairie Schooner
  Web; A Sense of Direction
Seattle Review
  Fox Squirrel
Sonora Review
  Someone Is Always Saying Something
Tar River Poetry
  Out of Sight; Things We Could Have Been; Morning Glory; How
  We See the Past
Tendril
  All There Is

Three Rivers Poetry Journal
　　Not the Right Place; What Doesn't Happen
Zone 3
　　Meditation for a New Moon; Young Amish Girl in Paradise

"Wishbone" is reprinted by permission from *New England Review and Bread Loaf Quarterly,* Vol. IX, No. 3, March 1987.

I would like to thank the National Endowment for the Arts for a fellowship that provided the time to help me complete this manuscript. I would also like to thank the Fulbright Foundation and its program through the Council for the International Exchange of Scholars which provided an opportunity to travel to Yugoslavia; this opportunity led to several of these poems. I also wish to thank the Faculty Research Committee at the University of Tennessee at Chattanooga for assistance. "Someone Is Always Saying Something" also appears in *Homewords,* an anthology of Tennessee writers.

Grateful acknowledgment is made for permission to quote from the following poems:
　　from Richard Hugo, "Distances," in *Making Certain It Goes On,* © 1984 by the estate of Richard Hugo. Used by permission of the publisher, W. W. Norton & Co.
　　from Randall Jarrell, "The Breath of Night" in *The Complete Poems,* © 1969 by Mrs. Randall Jarrell. Used by permission of the publisher, Farrar, Straus and Giroux.
　　from Theodore Roethke, "Journey to the Interior" in *Collected Poems of Theodore Roethke,* © 1966 by Beatrice Roethke as administratrix of the estate of Theodore Roethke. Used by permission of the publisher, Doubleday & Co.
　　from Wallace Stevens, "Esthetique Du Mal" in *The Palm at the End of the Mind,* ed. Holly Stevens, © 1971 by Holly Stevens. Used by permission of the publisher, Alfred Knopf, Inc.

The greatest poverty is not to live
In a physical world, to feel that one's desire
Is too difficult to tell from one's despair.

—Wallace Stevens

Contents

I

Here too, though death is hushed, though joy
Obscures, like night, their wars,
The beings of this world are swept
By the strife that moves the stars.
—Randall Jarrell, "The Breath of Night"

How Far the Light Travels

Sometimes we meet between
two words barely holding
the night together, or ourselves,
as tonight, waked by the cry of
a bird caught in the chimney,
the things we say become
our shadows. The bird's cry
makes the world outside
so near. It is possible
he is trapped, as we are, by a voice
that needs to contain everything,
the way each memory holds
another, somewhere inside it.
I remember being trapped in
a quarry one winter, the air
sagging, the ice the only
thing that kept Joey Stefano
and me from sinking, and on which
we misspelled our own names in
the panic that would dissolve later
as words do. Or later that spring,
following the silver skippers,
half moths, half butterflies,
as they darted in and out of
the sedge, in and out of ourselves,
to where he showed me the scar,
a long rope down his chest.
Sometimes, it is impossible to remember
any less than we want—walking
on coal cinders bubbled
hard beside the tracks, we played
until the dark became
heavy in the trees, the air

too heavy for his lungs. That is why
I have imagined the bird escapes,
not because it is right, or true,
but as the only gift I can bring you,
a gift that vanishes as the bird
vanishes, following a stream
back to its hidden source in
the marsh, and because tonight,
remembering the quarry and that boy
who would die alone, death
seems something that happens so many
times without us it becomes
as impossible as the light our window
lamp casts into shadows,
yet who knows how far any light
travels, even ours, across
the salt hay, across the spaces
we invent as we name our pasts.

Unable to Refuse

Some places we can't refuse. This is the night
I never arrived, never called, and even a few hours after
the storm the trees are trying to tell me things
I don't want to hear. The land around is empty with
sinkholes, what a chart on the wall says are
the slow crumblings of the limestone base. This is the place
where the earth sucks in fences, rusted hayrakers,
barns leaning on braces of 4 × 8's for a few years
to delay but not refuse geography. It's the farmers
who make best use of them—filling the holes with
garbage, cuttings, even old cars that disappear
after several months or years. Here the dirty earth
pulls in everything, covers it over, turns it into
itself, so you don't refuse anything, not even love.

At least that's what the woman at the end of the counter
tries to tell everyone here as long as the storm has kept us
together, and maybe she's right. At least it's a word
that gets taken in by others—the way it is spoken in
anything *sloven,* like the young drunk knocking hell
out of the condom machine in the trucker's restroom
planning to climb into some girl as if she were earth,
or even the beautiful *plover* that's just threatening to
                         re-emerge.

The newspaper the woman holds announces the death of the
                                   young
boy who re-emerged from his bubble chamber south of here:
"Bubble Boy Loses Battle in Dirty World," and really,
the world is dirty, at least here where the boy has never
been to refuse any earth, who has barely walked
on grass, never mind this sinking land.   [STANZA BREAK]

So this is the place
I've come to, trapped inside a truck stop until the earth
refuses or accepts me, keeping me from home, listening
to things I don't want to hear—the woman at the counter
talking about the boy and love in the same breath,
yet thinking how wrong it is to refuse anything after all,
and how, those times we refused each other, we seemed to
disappear.

Why We See What We See

for Gary Margolis

In another room my daughter is holding
a classroom globe and thinks the world
isn't so big. Maybe she's right.
Do you remember how, when we sat
one evening reading to each other,
the clouds gathered, darkened, and we joked
to imagine the power our words might hold?
Whatever we said, the wind said
again, south of there, where horizons
were visible and important. South of there is
here, where you asked about the bird
that sang, "don't you see?" "don't you see?"
We didn't, but my daughter says she can
see the other side of the world. Gary,
in the sound of that bird, we should've seen
another time or place. You asked its name—
the rufous-sided towhee, who nests
and scratches on the ground or low bushes,
and doesn't see much more than we do.
My daughter says we live in a place
larger than the world, if only we could see it.
I don't know, finally, what isn't invisible.
There's no time anywhere we can touch
which is exactly what that bird had to say.

Venus

So many roads end at this point
though, unlike us, they have no choice,
for the rest is sea, where we went yesterday
watching the humpback whales, descendants
of mammals who chose their way wisely
back to the sea, having become too heavy
for air to hold their soft bones together,

and where four of them lined up to our boat
just to remind us how little, that far
from land, we stood for, before edging away
leaving their fluke-like prints, oily roads on
the surface as they sounded. What they do below is
a mystery, though mating games and eating
bluefish and eels are what we think.

If we were not so limited we could hear them—
the sound of an orchestra warming up, random,
distant sounds, like ours for each other.
As long as the whales kept sounding,
sending up bubble clouds to trap
the eels, breaching to stun them loudly,
or rolling on their side, waving their fins,

this was a story about how near
they seemed and how we could learn from them
to rebegin, as they did, entering the sea.
So maybe it was no accident that Venus appeared,
who could have been the goddess for all I know,
or a broken statue in some museum—her tail
shredded, blubber hanging from a stump,   [STANZA BREAK]

raising it and slapping water, denying
how helpless we seemed. How helpless
we were last year when a humpback nearly
beached itself on the rocks: no one
knows why they sometimes drive towards
land as if they wanted to return from
where they began, suffocating from the weight

of their past. It is not by accident, either,
that a horseshoe crab, a creature older
than the whale, has caught its tail in a crevice
below, and will have to wait for the tide
to free it. Evolving slowly, it has learned
how to wait. And it is not by accident
I remember that as a boy we called its young

Venus crabs because their soft
shells are shaped like hearts. The first
things I killed were those tiny crabs
I sealed in a jar, myself too young
to know how they'd suffocate overnight,
though I remember still their putrid smell.
The smell of a beached whale is difficult

also to believe or endure. Venus,
the naturalist on board said, had a stump
that might putrify, infecting her. Or she would
go on, as lovers do, whether in myth
or in the ordinary waiting their lives demand,
whether whispering, or in these random, distant
sounds the humpbacks teach us to sing.

Young Amish Girl in Paradise

At first she is hardly visible
occupying the top left hand corner not just
because her plain black dress and bonnet are
merely a shadow in the open cab
or because the cornfields almost swallow
the buggy, but because I've been busy
trying to figure out what all these lark sparrows are
doing, there must be dozens,
flying in and out of this sycamore tree
so alive it seems to sing here topping a small hill.

I am told a blind man thinks of trees
when he thinks of size, for he knows
better than we can how endlessly the branches
extend beyond what he hopes to see.
These sparrows are not blind, but they are
smart enough to follow each branch
wherever it leads, yet cautious enough
to return, testing what they have found by touch.

Often as a boy I would hit stones out
with a bat from beneath such a sycamore,
making a large circle, extending a world
that was always too simply itself.

By now the girl has come so far
from home she is almost afraid.
When she arrives, she collects the brown and green
flakes of bark that have peeled from the trunk
and which are almost as thick as corn.
She must be very young for I see there may be
the faintest trace of color in her plain clothes.
She is not supposed to be here alone—

10

but I neglected to mention the young man
who's waiting in the carriage and whom
I would like to think we have both ignored.

My ignorance is not what stops me
from asking, for I know as well as she does
that the world she lives in is not so small,
that each morning she follows the unbroken
branches of these roads that lead beyond
this spot, beyond what she
or these lark sparrows have dreamt before.

Worlds Apart

I can't help but believe the killdeer,
so deftly has it led me,
dragging its own wings away from a poorly
hidden nest before clenching back into flight,
and I can't help but believe in a love
that would make itself so vulnerable for its young.

It is hard to understand, but
only by leaving do we know what we love.

Before I left, you told the story
of the fledgling cuckoo who hatches on a sparrow's
nest, who spills out the native fledglings,
and is adopted by the vulnerable parents.
One night, in a city far from home,
I watched in amazement as two young men
who seemed more fierce than the cuckoo,
stooped to kiss some bag lady on the forehead
and pass her a dollar, a lady who had nested on a corner
with her dozen sacks and a cart.

Never have I felt so guilty
for what little love I could show.
That night, alone on a bus, I thought
you were the starlight nesting in the trees
holding every moment of your life.

In the pine woods along the coast north of here
starlight never touches the ground.
Somewhere in there the cuckoo will begin to sing.
I don't think there was ever a time we weren't
approaching each other through those woods.
I don't think there is a moment we have

that is not taking place somewhere else,
or a love that doesn't lead us, sometimes
deftly, further from ourselves.

Wild Horses

"Life is probably round."
—Van Gogh

I may not have told you this,
but one night while we slept I dreamt
we stood among the wild horses of Assateague,
marooned as they were once, grown round
and small on salt grass. Another night,
it was the blind fish of Mammoth Cave
who have no sense of place and think
that their dark space is all the world.
And I am going to mention Pascal who loved
our blindness when he said, as blindly as anyone:
"Nature is an infinite sphere whose center
is everywhere and whose circumference is nowhere,"
which means that everything is the same place,
or that we live in places we imagine
for each other, so that it is all right
that we never go back. I have imagined
a place where we can hear the rain again
before it touches ground, where you can
hear the sounds of your childhood disguised
as the sounds of the cat waiting for birds
to approach the feeder. Most of these things
have nothing to do with us, we like to think,
hoping, really, that we can hide better
than our words that mean so many wrong things.
What I mean is: the perfect roundness
of your breasts, our lives, these days,
the perfect trust of one body in another.
These days the sky is big enough to put on,
as we hear someone say, and I believe it is.
And I believe the moon which also leaks

its damp light into the marsh. I believe
the single cricket trying to squeeze in under
my door as I write you from this place you have
already imagined. I believe that for years
I have touched you wherever I put out my hand.
I believe the wild horses of Assateague are beginning
to lift their heads, wondering at our slow approach,
knowing our distance by the sounds of crickets,
yet knowing how round the world is after all,
and perhaps they could know, those nights we loved so
blindly,
how we could also see, wherever we looked,
the endless places we will call our own.

Center Field

I don't think it will ever come down,
it flew so quickly beyond the small hollow
the field lights make in the approaching dusk,
and I begin to realize how uneven the outfield is—
the small holes that test your ankles, the slight pitch
towards deep center that makes backpedaling so risky
but keeps pulling you as if further into your past.

It must be falling out of another world,
'lint from the stars' we used to say on a sandlot
in Lawrence, Mass.—and I have so much time
to imagine what you will say between innings
about what we try to steal from our darkening pasts,
how age means knowing how many steps we have lost,
remembering that too many friends have died,
and how love is the most important thing,
if only we knew who to love, and when.

The ball is just becoming visible again
and I am trying to remember anyone I have loved,
and it turns out it was usually too late, that we stood
like embarrassed batters caught looking at a third strike.
Yet somehow in this long moment I have slid
past the outstretched arms of twenty years,
and I can see Joey Gile crouched at third base
waiting, as it happened, for the bullet of some sniper
to snap like a line drive into his chest,
for John Kearns to swing and miss everything
from a tree in his back yard and not be found
for two days, for Joe Daly, whom I hardly knew
and who hardly had time to steal away
when the tractor slipped gear and tagged him to a tree,
for Gene Coskren who never understood baseball

and was fooled by a hit and run in Syracuse, N.Y.,
and somehow I am going to tell them all.

And my mother's sister who loved this game
and who complained for years about her stomach,
the family joke, until the cancer struck
and she went down faster than any of them.
And her own aunt, "I don't want to die," she said, and slid
her head to the pillow not out of fear
but embarrassment, stranded, she thought,
with no one to bring her home, no one to love.

But in the meantime, look, this is a poem
that could go on being about either death or love,
and we have only the uncertain hang time
of a fly ball to decide how to position ourselves,
to find the right words for our love,
to turn towards home as the night falls, as the ball,
as the loves, the deaths we grab for our own.

Blue Moon

The morning I left, the rain stopped,
and I found the nest of a yellow warbler
five layers deep, each layer holding
the egg of a cowbird the warbler covered
to protect its own fledglings, the way,
you said, we hide those feelings that threaten

whatever we love. It must have fallen
from a sapling, heavy with its past and the rain.
It broke apart in my hands. A pair of
warblers flashed low around me, afraid,
as they are, of too much sky. One night,
the sky shrunken by mountains and far

clouds, we watched a blue moon
lower itself between trees as gently as any
lover. When the clouds covered the stars
you read our history in, I didn't understand
you were afraid, or what you meant by saying
too much water in our signs is what makes us so alone.

I thought of that this evening where I have stood
alone on the shore south of you, following
the lights of boats, they could almost be stars,
searching for an injured whale that has entangled
itself with fishing line. I thought of the whale
you described trapped in the shallow bay

near you. Somewhere at sea, its mate
would have waited till the end. Did you know
that the female will hold the male away
for hours by holding herself perfectly vertical?

Perhaps they know better than we do
when to hide and when to reveal their love.

Tonight, the moon is no longer blue,
and the truth is that its blueness is a legend
to describe its fullness twice in one month.
The truth is, the moon is as yellow as those warblers.
Under it, an aging man has been waiting with
his lover, even older, who has suffered a stroke.

They, too, are watching the far boats. He has
brought her a stuffed animal and brushes back
her hair with a touch that must also be a blessing,
that brings them to a past far from here.
They have come to know that all time falls finally
around us, as that nest did, as the rain did,

as the light from those stars you tried to chart,
a light that begins in so many other places.
The light from this moon, blue or yellow,
holds a few birds low over the water.
I think the light of this earth, our own light,
has already gone out to whomever we have loved.

This is why—knowing finally what your stars meant,
what that nest meant beyond the sad death of love—
this is why I bless these lovers, bless you,
afraid to touch anyone, bless the blue
moon that says how rare any love is
that hides from itself so fully what it fears.

The Promise of Light

In the background, steam rises from the snow patches,
and from the backs of horses nearly out of sight
yet making their way towards a hidden stream.
For a moment, the crowd that is gathered around the man
who drank himself to death does not know whether
to look at this and the other pictures he painted
at the end of this alley in perfect detail, or at the man.

I believe the artist painted his scenes from Gustav Mahler's
Pastoral, and it must be that by now the horses
would have found the stream, so much do they seem to trust
the artist's stroke which allows them all to turn
away, perhaps from shyness. Once, north of Atlanta,
I came upon two trailers in a wreck that had spilled
their horses, quiet and unnatural, on the wet pavement,

lit at intervals by the blue lights of the police cruisers.
No doubt these horses waiting to disappear into
the wall are those horses alive in a world we can't name,
and this man, who kept a photograph of a woman he never
knew, cut from a magazine, as his friends explain,
speaking his whole life to her, invented whatever
past, whatever future, he could trust to face the dark.

And surely he remembered, for the first time in years,
climbing the ladder down to the bottom of a pier—
the stars already fading—with a girl he hardly
knew, the wooden pilings coated with barnacles
and black seaweed, the tide low, the oil slicks
gathering on the harbor around driftwood, paper
cups, tin cans, dead fish—gathering towards

the darkness which was the other shore they swam for,

trusting luck, trusting the certainty of tides. He must
have remembered how long it takes to trust anything.
I remember reading how Mahler as a boy watched until
                                                    dawn,
not believing in the burlap bags stuffed with the hair
of mice and human hair—charms his uncle hung
around the orchard because nuisance deer couldn't stand the
                                                    smell.

Now, in silence, the crowd begins to break up. The artist
who had seemed only to be sitting asleep on a cinder
block he took from an empty lot next door is gone,
and I almost believe the fog on the walls might lift,
revealing the scene I read once where Mahler watched,
from a distance, a girl so awkwardly beautiful he couldn't
trust what he saw. The man with her lifted her blouse

and placed it across a branch, its arms spread
like antlers, or spread like the arms of another lover,
or her father, or even Mahler becoming too slowly the man
who would finally understand that whoever you love is
all of a sudden there, promising nothing but the next day,
the way fireflies would gather as they all began
to leave, promising nothing but their own brief light.

In those days, the imprints from tie beams in the shadow
of a railbed in Bohemia would be enough to take him
                                                    anywhere.
Once, by tracks like those, I found and broke open a brown
                                                    cocoon—
inside were hundreds of yellow spiders entangled in each
other's lives, the way our own lives and the lives
of so many we never knew, even this poor artist's,
become entangled by whatever stories we remember.

I remember the story of Gustav Mahler writing
his pastoral symphony in a world as silent as this wall,

instructing his wife to untie the bells from cows,
cut the rope to the village tower, teach singers
how to mime—and how she would try to silence the birds,
                                                        keep
the horses from running—and how, later, he would lock
                                                    himself
in a room waiting for his daughter to die, and how he would
                                                    return

to the Danube to face his own lingering death. And I
                                    remember
Mike Connally, the sketch artist who played left field
with an old, stubby glove and whom we called "Sky" because
                                                    of the long
fly balls he'd hit, and how he turned away, in the end, from
any sky to face the quiet of the Tennessee for three weeks
                                                    before
they found him. I think he knew what the poet Delmore
                                    Schwartz meant
by the deafness of solitude, the world we are never able to
                                                    hear—

Schwartz, who wrote on a restroom wall in Syracuse,
                                    New York,
"Give me $5 and the change and I'll go where the morning
and the evening can't hurt me," and who lay finally
for three days in a New York City morgue. We live
so seldom in the real world, he said, because we are
so often surprised by the deaths of friends, and cannot
understand, even from that, the meaning of our own deaths.

It may be that now I no longer wish to tell one event
from another, believing the stars which are moving away
yet reappear, like the stories of this artist, of Mahler, of
                                    Schwartz,
and of Mike Connally. On the far wall is a picture of wolves
who must have stalked a caribou to death for weeks,

trusting, even as the artist must have, in the terrible
meaning of that event, trusting, as we must, in the way

the mind and heart find each other out
despite our own fears, despite whatever details
we invent to divert ourselves, these stories or images
we make of the morning emerging from the fog where,
when we look carefully, one or the other of us is
also emerging, trusting whatever silence lingers,
knowing the world begins from where we are.

The Waterfall

I believe you, our prayers never end.
I received your photographs of spiders' webs
that blur the soapbush, the telephone lines,
fields of goldenrod—a species that has learned
to live in colonies more social
than the poor country you write from.

On those streets, more than once,
a young man, his life draining from him,
has been stopped by some war or another,
has tried to climb out of whatever lay
invisible in the dirt, to find a single prayer
that meant the earth would shrug him off alive.

Today, beside the mist of our waterfall
wavering like one of those webs in the wind,
I have learned what those frogskins we used to find
abandoned on the rocks must mean.
They mean a waterbug the size of your thumb
has stung them, paralyzed and dissolved their
bones and organs, and sucked them dry.
That is the only way to see such a thing.
In the end, everything dissolves into
words like *fear* and *loss*,
words we pray with, hoping it's enough.

I have learned this tonight while
the invisible eggs of walking-sticks drop from maples
making a sound that could be a far waterfall.
Believe me, that sound could almost be a prayer.
How could it be anything else?
I say all this because you asked
before you left where a waterfall ends,

and I have learned little else except
a waterfall ends inside us, dissolving in
whatever prayer of ours the earth will believe or accept.

What Doesn't Happen

In 1954 my grandmother told me,
holding a violet chicory flower, that the color
could be indigo or blue, depending on the way I was
taught to name the spectrum. I have been thinking of her
this afternoon, watching the soaring motions of a distant
sparrow hawk until it turned out to be a crow.

In 1954 I was the boy on the other
side of the Shawsheen River
out of sight of the couple becoming good
vines to each other, coming home to
my grandmother's spacious house, watching the crazy
chickens flap a few feet in the air trying
to follow the geese towards Canada, and later
my grandmother slapping imaginary bats out of
the cellar with a straw broom.

In 1954 the sets of French doors
opened into endless rooms, the bannister
disappearing into the upper floors
where at the keyhole of her room I could hardly
believe my grandfather's skin wrinkled like a brown
paper bag, or his consolations to her, holding her hand
already shaking from Parkinson's disease,
could hardly understand the slow love they made
half out of the keyhole's range.

Maybe the world is everything we don't see—
this walking-stick disguised as an oak twig
or leaf stalk, waiting to flick at its prey,
the green frog camouflaged on a mossy rock.
If only we knew where to look, and for what!

Wishbone

"Perhaps poetry, instead of being the rather meaningless
transmutation of reality, is a combat with it; and perhaps the
thing to do when one keeps saying that life is a dull life is to
pick a fight with reality."

—Stevens

"In one of my poems that is successful, there is much more
reality than in any relationship or affection that I feel."

—Rilke

This could be the poem you picked from the ruins,
the day the air was so thick with the must of the past
one word as simple as *love* could have changed the story.
This is a poem so reluctant to reveal how it arrived there
or to face the outside world, it tries to talk only
to itself. In fact, this sentence is telling you that
its hero is really Cervantes, the poor son of a noble
doctor, who visited court each time a swordsman
needed mending, Cervantes, the soldier of fortune,
wounded at Lepanto, taken prisoner by pirates,
who knew his own hero, Don Quixote, not by the comic
surface, but by his desire to avoid the tragic
pain just underneath. It would like to reflect
on the way Don Quixote, later in his own fiction,
must play the role his early story has made.

Or, this could be the poem I handed you when we visited
the ruined Church Tower, its library shelves covered
with bird droppings, a scene, you said, that was written
for Cervantes. This was the tiny wishbone of a sparrow
you found in the ruins. I kept it for luck, and for love.
Later, the poem intends to tell you where I lost it,
to tell you the far places it has been, the stories it heard,
but now there is something it can no longer avoid. [STANZA BREAK]

For a while this poem began with Rodrigo Rojas
who was caught on the streets of Santiago, Chile, beaten
to the ground with rifle stocks along with his companion,
doused with gasoline and burned, then covered with a
                                                    blanket,
dumped in a ditch so that death would come more slowly.
This is not the story the poem wanted to face. It does
not want to see Rodrigo, a bystander, does not want to
focus on his eyes in the first puzzle of dying,
does not want to feel the fire in his throat, unable
to talk for the few bad days in the local hospital.
It would rather skip a few lines to the cafe where
no one has yet heard the news. It would rather argue
that when you are not reading them, none of these lines
remembers him anyways. The girls in the bar are laughing.
"Include me in one of your poems," one says, "but do not
mention my name." "If I were you," another laughs,
"who would be saying this?" If I were you.
The poem is having trouble thinking only of itself.
At the funeral of Rodrigo Rojas it took four militiamen
of President Augusto Pinochet to hold the water cannon
that would dissolve the procession. It would take hours
for the frightened people to flee the safety of the church
like swifts pouring from the bell tower at evening.

From the tower of our own church we could see far
                                                    mountains
through the greasy windows, and a yellow bird, a warbler,
I believe, blurred on the maple branch wondering at our
                                                    silence.
The poem fumbles here awkwardly to tell you how
one night, the next week, I swore it was the same
bird's song that lit the far darkness of Belgrade
so that I woke dreaming of you, and went down to the street
and found an old man from the hospital, in a bathrobe,
also unable to sleep, and for a long while we watched the
                                                    water

truck spray the street drowning out the sound of that lonely
bird. "We are here," he said, "because we know that memory
must stop inviting guests from the past. You have to forget,
as this truck does, all the scraps of the day—the gum
wrappers, popsicle sticks, straws. We will look
at anything, a street worker, a building project, a traffic
policeman, anything mindless to stop from remembering.
Even so, there is a scene or two that escapes. It returns
like a prisoner. It remembers one night, the rain endless,
the artillery flashes beyond the ridges. The difficulty
in raising your boots out of the mud. It remembers the old
comrades, the blankets rolled like seashells where
no sea sounded. The next day the Germans entered
Kragujevac, the old battle ground against the Turks,
to shoot the seven thousand men and boys." After a while,
the old man was all pipe smoke and leaned into the past
of Kragujevac which was the past of his own son,
leaned into the wall, as his own son must have.
But the truth is, he must have imagined the thousand
ways death could come, what the boy must have thought.
This poem would like to report Kragujevac is the only place
it happened, though it remembers another town, nameless,
where still, out of respect, no men are allowed to enter.
Instead, it will tell you we watched the truck disappear
across the scraps of two languages, the men lit by the red
light in the cab, and by the light of their own cigarettes.
If Quixote were there. The old man could have been
Cervantes and the truck would have stood for the dragons
of everything he feared, everything he couldn't understand.

I showed him the wishbone then, and I remembered the
                                                    stories
you could imagine for how it came there, for what lovers
had stolen off to that tower, hiding behind the books.
There was a young girl, just married, who hid there
fearing love, collapsing into the wide hoops of her gown.
I believed you. And I believe that the bird, whatever it was

breaking the Belgrade night, has never stopped, that the
                                                        poem
takes that persistent song as an elegy, wonders what bird
sang above the crowds in Santiago the day of the burning,
remembers the birds of the tower, the signal birds
Quixote woke to, the birds of every elegy continuing.
The poem, though, does not want to be an elegy.
It has already become impatient with its theory of place:
how a Church tower in Tennessee a few months ago
can become also a tower in Belgrade almost anytime.
It wants instead to deal only with single things:
the yellow bird on the branch, balancing the wind,
unable to decide to fling its soul out, and to whom.
Waiting five years in a prison for ransom, Cervantes,
too, would listen to the birds that sang of freedom.
On the walls of the cell he would etch a few poems.
I don't have to tell you the poems of Rodrigo Rojas are
written everywhere. They are poems we find in ruins.

Even in Belgrade. I stood in the rain at the great fort's tower,
I stood where the Roman legions watched the barbarians
gather on the plains across the Danube, I stood where
the Partisans watched the German *Stukas* dive unannounced
from the sky. I stood in the rains that came from Chernobyl,
and I fingered the wishbone for luck. The next day
I would head for Zagreb where, years ago, in the first light
of St. Mark's square, watching a few women hugging the sills
of houses along the walk to the bakery, the trees scorched,
hearing the rail cars begin, the traitor Pavelic offered
to his German friends another basketful of human eyes.
No one wanted to look. No one wanted to glance up
from the tasks of finding eggs or cleaning the streets.
Pavelic only smiled. The gray coat and trousers,
the gray muddied boots said nothing was unusual.
Nothing unusual, the poem says, where centuries earlier,
in that same square, the hero of the peasant revolt
was awarded a red hot iron crown, dismembered, and burned.

                                                [STANZA BREAK]

So now the poem does not know who to trust.
It could trust the old man in Belgrade, and perhaps
he really was Cervantes who admitted in the end the failure
of all dreams, and who has now gone back to his room
to take a little *mandarina* and crackers with the dawn.
Somewhere in Belgrade, the gypsy children are washing
windows at intersections, one hand stuffed with rags,
the other holding out for a few dinars. The old women,
kerchiefs tight around their heads, are dreaming for the huge
sides of lamb in the butcher windows. It is not raining.
The young men walk the promenade, stopping for beer.
This is where the poem wants to linger, lifting a glass.
It wants to tell Don Quixote's episode in the Inn.
Instead, it recalls the cafe in Santiago. A little
girl is carrying an apron full of flowers which she sells
for nearly as much as they cost. Her straight black hair
hangs unevenly and needs to be combed. It is expected
that she has no shoes, that her parents have been taken,
but the poem is too polite to ask. Behind her, a troop
carrier clatters past. The poem is getting nervous.
It wants to find a home for you in one of its sentences.
It wants to tell a story with a few touching mementos.

I began, tonight, by trying to tell you I still have
the wishbone, to tell you about this river, however
moonless the night, the surface touched by *skaters*,
or what they call in Texas, Jesus Bugs, walking
their simple miracles on water. But what I have taken
to be skaters might be the reflection of a plane's light
on the surface, or a car's, or the few expected stars.
The poem doesn't care, finally, what we call them.
It does not want the unexpected, though it makes me
remember, because of the skaters, another season
where my friend followed the sled tracks of his daughter
to a pond's edge, early thaw, and drowned
going after her. I think it has to do with the way the heart
tries to understand its own losses by those of others.

It has to invent those lives to live. I remember
my own daughter, chasing pigeons, opening her arms
as if to gather them all in as they rose around her,
dozens of them. Even now, she too, embraces most
what flies away. For a few hours now we have
stood where the Annisquam river becomes sea and she is
watching a harbor seal bring its secrets to the surface every
few yards. I must tell you I have cast the wishbone,
as the Portuguese fishermen do, on this tidal river, for luck,
hoping to keep a while a few friends from the sky,
for the old man in Belgrade, for the memory of Rodrigo Rojas.
I must tell you this poem has put no boats upon the water,
no lobster boats with their signal lights redeeming
what the sea will take, no boats of lovers edging
their way into the coves, paint scaling from the sides,
the oars too loud in anticipation, not because they do not
belong there, but because remembering all these,
remembering how you knew the lives that haunted the tower,
surely you too would have suffered the losses this poem has
failed to replace, surely you have imagined already the boats.

II

As a blind man, lifting a curtain, knows it is morning,
I know this change:
On one side of silence there is no smile;
But when I breathe with the birds,
The spirit of wrath becomes the spirit of blessing
And the dead begin from their dark to sing in my sleep.
                    —Theodore Roethke, "Journey to the Interior"

For the Nameless Man at the Nursing Home near the Shawsheen River

Sometimes you step into the river twice
and it's the same river. The sky leans
down just to show the importance of sky.
Boys on the bridge are throwing rocks,
carelessly, at elusive carp in the changeless river.
They do not think of the love they have never known.

Today my daughter tells me how each pail of river
water holds nearly invisible worlds of life—
larvae, rotifers, algae, plankton, sponges,
diatoms, protozoa, seed shrimp.
It's as if each thing we have is another thing,
each moment we have, another moment.

There's no telling this
to the old man smoking his white clay pipe,
its stem so long he has to keep his hand
extended as if to offer or accept a gift.
He is telling the best tales that will make
sense of his past that seems so much longer
than his own life—one son's final letter
inventing a fragile world from some jungle,
another son's absent letters stuffing his pockets.

I am not going to tell him
some allegory to bring him back to this moment
by pointing to the praying mantis on the railing
mounted by her mate from behind, turning
a shoulder to clutch it around the neck,

devouring its head even as they continue.
There's no sense telling him that her mate's
protein, not love, is what sustains her,
or to try imagining her mate knows all this beforehand.

I am just going to sit here with
this old man I hardly know, but who I am
going to say is my own father
whom I have denied long enough, the terrible
secret of sons, because it is true that
to fill the spaces between steps with love is
to empty yourself, to become the perfect lie
giving back the gift of emptiness, the perfect
emptiness of the river which holds everything,
what those boys knew—that there is
almost nothing that does not mean love,
however elusive, and that the loves we abandon
and the loves we keep are the same love.

Not the Right Place

for Bernie

The redpolls this March are far south where they shouldn't
be,
tearing apart dried flower stalks for the hidden seeds,
the dream of spring they trust will bring them home.

Here and now, a first spring spider is falling
past me, towards anywhere on the wind which turns out
to be *from* a tulip poplar, the kind pioneers
would hollow out for canoes to carry them everywhere
and *towards* a moss pool where mosquitoes will later
emerge from rafts of eggs.

                    The trouble is, we dream
everything happens where we aren't. That's what
                        the shotgun
dents in the roadsigns leading nowhere tell me.
That's what the two young boys caught last night
on the school fire escape would say, trying
to make love to each other, scared by their loneliness.

My grandmother, whenever a relative would die,
hung out a set of clothes for the deceased to claim
or not, as custom had it, watched them shift in
the windy branches.

                    Bernie, there's no telling
at what cost all this has come. I have let
these images of flowers, spiders, legends intrude
because I was afraid, because I have discovered, hearing
again the crazy rattle of the redpoll, that shy
bird so easy to forget, so trusting it could be

kept, that for thirty years I had pretended you had moved,
not died, but the boy in that undersized casket
was you, which I still hope to deny, saying you are
here, a simple matter of place after all, as if
I could hang these hopes out for you to fill.

Raspberries

"For thinking and Being are the same. For that reason, all these will be mere names which mortals have laid down, convinced that they were true: coming-to-be as well as passing away, Being as well as nonbeing, and also change of place and variation of shining color."

—Parmenides

"There are no Dead . . . the Grave is but our moan for them."
—Emily Dickinson, *Letters*, Feb. 1870

The old man knows the earth is not a dream.
He is not going to read my poem about the tiny
brown and yellow saw-whet owl, silent,
as it often is by day behind the flute sounds
of my daughter's practice, nor will he listen to any
self-indulgence about whether it cares if I'm here.

Instead, he is stockpiling old painkillers
to prescribe the time of his own death. This morning,
the old man showed me his palms stained like a map
by raspberries he was selling, and I remembered how
I used to believe that the souls of suicides wandered
a geography not even Parmenides could name.
He wasn't going to say what he believed. He wasn't
going to tell his wife when the pain became too great.
Behind him, the cracks in the window frames of his shack
were stuffed with wads of paper to keep the hornets
and wasps from going after the berries, and I could see,
still, my own father, how he'd protect the preserves
in our cellar—peach, strawberry, grape, raspberry,
blueberry, holding the whole summer by stockpiling
the sunlight, he'd say, for the winter's dark cold,
the winter's silence.   [STANZA BREAK]

41

But this old man, he wasn't
going to hold on to the past, he only wanted to talk about
how the earth had fallen apart along that coast, the glaciers
rotted from the insides, trailing the long gravel beds
down the sides of hills, how the walls of those cliffs
tell us the life we have is only a few centimeters in rock.

He wasn't going to read my poem, but I have left him in
here, sitting with a few wooden boxes at his roadside
stand. And why not? I don't know any longer what will be
important—tonight my daughter rushed in here
from practicing with news her friend's heart had suddenly
failed. I wanted the stain of a father's love to hold
longer than I knew it would. What could I tell her?
A few years ago, when legend, not geography, held us,
I would tell her the Indian stories for death—
how the father of Shining Waters was the Sun,
how her young lover saved her father's home
dispelling the birds of darkness by his own death.
I had forgotten until now how we have to invent
a life for the dead.

                    I had doubted, when I began,
that Parmenides was right to say that what we thought
became the world we lived, but when you look
carefully, markings set by men or time in rocks,
objects in legends or poems, tell you whatever story
you want them to. This morning I believed it was
only a question of not using such a tired symbol
of loneliness and despair as that owl. Now,
as my daughter reads the notes they passed
in school, their children's jokes, the message to remember
Jennifer whenever she played, she is trying to find
the words to hold her close.

                    Do you know what I'm saying?
I am trying to find for her what secret words

preserve our pasts, what secret brings the owl back
again to these lines where it doesn't seem to belong.
I had seen it before. Years ago, the woman across
the unpaved street that would be covered late that summer,
the same woman who was beating an old Persian rug
she'd strung across the cast iron bars of the clothesline,
looked up and saw the small owl that must have tangled
itself in the rope lines. She looked up and knew the cancer
deep in her liver, knew, I believe, it would take her in a week.
In those days, when we ate bread soaked in milk,
when we bottled rootbeer in sarsaparilla bottles and waited
for the street to be paved or tarred, while the neighborhood
grew and the owls disappeared, I held my mother, afraid
that she, too, might die. It was the summer we walked
along the railroad tracks picking raspberries for miles
of happiness, hearing my father scratch a song on the
                                    harmonica
trying to make us forget the woman whose name is lost now,
and the boy who would ride his bike beneath the tar truck,
his face burned to a mask, and the neighbor who parachuted
into the Korean sea, all the faces that return now faster
than I want them to.

        So this is it, this is why I am
going to include all this in that old poem for another summer,
as Parmenides would, why I am going to let the owl,
then or now, speak for whatever future rises from the trees,
itself rising, as Parmenides does in the fragments of his own
lost poem, to escape the geography of grief, the dark
that gathers, anyways, failing what we hoped for it,
why I am going to tell the old man how any breath,
however pained, is what Jennifer would choose, why I am
going to listen to the sound of my daughter's flute
rising like the old legends, setting like a stain in the air,
as the owl lifts a wing, as we all move off, becoming
a few lines in the rock, holding whatever stories
keep us safe, into the silent worlds we hold so dear.

43

Morning Glory

She lived in a place where distance
began, testing yellow jackets the way
her grandmother taught her, covering
their hole in a muddy bank with a glass bowl
so they'd fly for a while confused
aiming for a sky too clear to ever reach.

Or she would be looking at skaters,
small insects on the surface of the water
tracing another face over hers,
and beneath, minnows filling her hair
and the pink and blue flowers
that seemed to bloom, reflected there, in
a world she was about to enter or to leave.

Later the smoke would nudge up through
the first shadows, and she would return
downstream to where her family,
there from the north country, camped those few
weeks to harvest apples, migrants for whom
the landscape was an afterthought, like hope.

I say this because she taught me
the first name I remember for a flower,
morning glory, a flowering vine whose roots
begin far from the blossoms, whose heart-shaped leaves
I thought would hold the sun forever,
and because this evening, glimpsing
the face of a girl who stood alone for a moment
amidst the crowd on a street far from that past,
I thought I saw again the underside of those petals.

I had forgotten she believed in a heaven

filled with those flowers. Evenings like this
the sky tries to show you everything
at once. Maybe there is only
one thing in the world we need to heal us,
some first star that claims the whole sky.
Or this flower I had picked in a field
years from here, held in my wallet to spend
when my love would grow so poor,
this morning glory which blooms on the breath
which is our first flowering,
and so returns whatever has been missing,
clinging wherever it will.

No Place to Hide

After a while I can see
the child beside the woman who is
too heavy to sit except with her legs
splayed out revealing the dark stocking
tops that grab too tightly above the knees is
not a child at all, but a young woman
whose arms and legs are the tiny wings
and fins we associate with birds and fish.

I have tried to watch only the woman rising
as if she could forget this is only the small
park by the hospital with its nameplate trees,
where the chestnut burrs are waiting to split
open late in the fall, from chestnut trees
a blight has long killed except in these parks
but whose sprouts continue everywhere from roots
until the blight pulls them back, too. Now she is
approaching the boy selling sausage
and the twisted pretzels he bakes in a small oven,
and who cares nothing for the history of these trees.
On the bench she has left a photo album
that she and the young girl were smiling
over. But what did they see there, or in this scene
which has itself become a kind of picture?

Once I found in an abandoned farmhouse
hundreds of pictures of women in strange costumes
some photographer had abandoned because
each turned out to be the same endless desire.
No one had dreamt for years over the telephone lines
sagging from that house to a few poles
and trees that could have been chestnuts.
Not even the sparrows could hope

for the gentle touch of voices through their feet.
But those were women I could safely touch, and did.

It is getting harder not to mention the young woman.
"You might as well ask the clouds
to hold their shapes," is what she says,
calling me, and I see that her photos are
all of clouds but labeled *blouse*,
cup, purse, carriage, shoe,
a world of things that become whatever shapes
they seemed to her the moment her friend's shutter clicked.

When I touch her goodbye
I think I am the father in one of her imaginary
pictures, holding an infant dressed too warmly,
who is looking away, perhaps frowning,
but the child is laughing for she alone has seen
the great thunderheads beyond the borders
that everyone else will have forgotten.

With the Woman in a Coma

She is there again, if the sudden flinch of her arm
can be trusted. No one knows whether the river is
isolated among pines, or how often she goes there,
or even if there is a river. But all I can ever

imagine when I am near her is that she is there,
dusk, quiet. She is sitting at the edge of a wharf
letting her careful feet dangle, not fishing
for minnows with dough and a small hook as I would.

I'm not sure why she's alone, no reflection, no boats.
But I know that she waits here for the minnows
to crease the water, their sound falling out of the night.
She is just sitting, dreaming of another place,

perhaps where the river began, what rain, what lake.
No one knows where that is either. No one is
going to wake her. Beneath the wharf the minnows
have been as motionless as the stones, white, rust,

she dreams with. The otters are coming to the water,
the deer are beginning to step cautiously from woods,
yet she must be further back, a little girl waiting
for vinegar and baking soda to clean her copper

cup. Her parents are worried she spends so much
time dreaming. Sometimes she walks to the river
alone just when the light is peeling from the water.
The current is too deep to notice. No one will tell her

not to disturb the minnows. That is when she wants to say
something is wrong, when she flinches. I can't stop
her awful recognition that the minnows beneath the wharf
could be her own cells swimming away from her.

From the Fort Payne, Alabama, Flea Market

The mother leaned over the cement
window sill of the orange brick tenement
and called to one son below, hobbling,
one leg longer than the other, and ignored
the other son who collected knives
and pictures of Christ in a room no one entered.
All day she watched the freighters move
up and down the Hudson, desperate to leave
for Miami or San Juan, where things were better.

I had forgotten about all this until now,
looking at the displays of knives, holy pictures,
and at these figurines, hundreds set out on tables,
the kind the mother collected to imagine
the places they came from: Torino, Barcelona, Trieste.

And I can't let it go now, and remember
how the mother kept calico asters in the window
planter because the unpredictable colors
told her anything could be true. The son would not
die in some street fight, and perhaps
I would take one of the lovely daughters
to a different life. That was long ago
and it never occurred to me to ask then
how those wild flowers appeared in the middle of the city.

Here, at the tables, everything is supposed to make you
think you could be anywhere. Clothes handed down
from another continent, guns from another war,
reed flutes from the hills, baskets from the delta.
Sometimes you have to be able to believe
you could hold your whole life again, start over. [STANZA BREAK]

That is why we are so fascinated with the stories
told by those who have come back after the doctor
has disconnected the machines and taken off his gloves.
Sometimes they see whomever they loved who died,
perfectly at rest, perhaps sitting at a window,
the wind barely exploring the ends of the flowers,
or they are startled to discover what they have felt,
whom they have loved from such a distance all that time.

That is why, taking your hand, I looked at you
across the table, unable to let go—because I was
startled to remember how much I have loved you.
And here, the album a woman is selling is all pressed
asters: yellow, purple, white, red. These are
blossoms someone years ago touched and did not want—
through all the deaths, the fevers, through whatever
wars and scant times, whatever darkness, whatever
poverty of heart—did not want ever to let go.

The Green Heron

Sometimes we disguise too well
what we want to say, as the herons
disguise themselves along
this shore almost becoming
grass. What a small time
we inhabit what we say! I know
a heron is not going to inhabit
the grass beyond his desire
for the wind. Maybe his cry
has wandered through the woods until
it surrounded this time that's small
enough to hold. Five years
ago I held my friend,
a soldier years from Asia
where the heron's call meant
another death in the marshes.
For him, just lying down on
the rusted springs of a queen
mattress at the city dump was
enough, hoping the gulls,
even twenty miles inland,
would leave him alone, whose voice was
the ruins of towns he'd known.
He spilled a grocery sack of
medals, photos, clippings,
rings, used dreams
that helped him name the dark.

Look, I began with a bird
I don't see, a man whose best
words were silent, not to tell
you about them, but about the woman
he couldn't forget killing

because he thought the fruit
she carried were disguised grenades.
Vistas rise behind whatever
we say or see. I wanted to tell
how deep the dark was when we spoke,
and that the moonlight filled
the scrub pine, but I can't say
such an elegy any longer,
though I can tell you how
the heron finally rises,
how it seems to take us with it,
drawing our own breath
in its loud rasp, and then
our pasts which surely we become
beyond our desire for them.

Three Elegies in the Same Place

1. Elegy with Birds for Russ Vliet

No one will know until tomorrow if the story
this time is true, so I will begin with the nuthatch
you loved, hacking open the hickory nuts,
not *hatching* as we have softened it to say,
and second cousin to the brown creeper, heard late
in winter or spring, whispering upwards before falling
to the base of the next tree. This is the elegy
just in case. This is the elegy of the wind
that has been approaching all this time from the hills.
It is not saying anything you don't know. It is just
beginning to nudge the brushfires where the fields are
being cleared. Perhaps we will want to sit
transfixed like a boy who stares at the flame and all
he sees is flame, because it holds him, because
it knows later, the ash becoming earth, when he looks
up, he will see that the field is only field.
Suppose he knows about the nuthatch and creeper,
birds who survive by doing one thing well,
themselves. Suppose he understands how anything is only
itself, but that we have within us pieces of everything.
Nuthatch, creeper, walking in nervous circles,
or flying downwards as if to say that at a certain
height everything turns into sky or nothing.
Suppose the boy is thinking of a distant place
beginning to spread its wings in his lungs. Suppose
he becomes all he says he will. The fields are
nearly clear. Someone is missing. And you,
suppose you look up, late winter, and you whisper.

53

2. *Elegy for the End of the Road*

You can't get there from here anymore.
The wind wasn't the wind at all
but the heat rising, trapped under
large leaves of some tropical plant, growing
dark. And the ground wasn't ground either,
only the roots and fallen branches criss
crossing like hundreds of gun sights
just over the forest floor. No one wanted to stop.
No one was going any farther. Joey Giles was
just going to rest, and maybe he was going
to think about trying to teach me again
how to hit a curve ball if only I would
step up in the batter's box. And except
for the sniper's bullet getting past him
as nothing had before, maybe he did. Then the wind
wanted to be something else. Then the ground
wouldn't give way for anything. No one was
going anywhere. Whatever was left to be said was
waiting in a place no one had yet thought of.
Even now you can't tell. It is always another
place. Where do you think, now, we have
been? Do you think we will get where we are going?

3. *The Elegy of Apologies*

Please forgive my writing this elegy for you.
No word of yours has reached me here for too long.
The small boats are empty, and toss about.
Someone, a child, pours sand from one fist
into her open palm, and then back again.
There is little else to talk about here.
The grass is tall enough. Here are the insects
beginning to make again the song of your leaving.
Here are the parasitic wasps laying their eggs

in the air to avoid being devoured by their larvae.
Here are the delicate, beautiful lacewings
laying their eggs on leaves and devouring them.
Even the future seems to have deserted itself.
Here are the old men waiting at the edges
of piers. Now we will see if they can hear
the river buoy clang when the wind picks up.
I have heard you have had some difficult times.
I have heard they took away the emptiness
of your hands so that you no longer reach
for anything. Forgive me. There is nothing here.
Please forgive me for calling this elegy yours.

How We See the Past

We were only standing there, gazing blankly
beside the Ashley river in Charleston
where Adam Bennett was nearly hung
by Union forces for protecting
the hiding place of his master's silver.
In a little while we would be
startled by the dozens of crows
shifting between palm trees
calling us out beyond ourselves,
and we would notice the "cypress knees,"
those ugly roots surfacing for air
from the black water. Sometimes
we stand so much in the past
the past is all we see.

Beyond us, no one wanted to notice
the radio's news of another bombing,
or the gaze of the young black men
a few miles from here, stationed
outside a store front waiting
to exchange their pints of blood for cash.

The fear our own lives may be lost,
not cruelty, is what turns us away
toward a past we barely see to hold.

Beside a river like this
I cut peat moss with my father,
the rich air nearly overcoming us,
and later, beside a smaller stream
near his nursing home I watched
a blind woman move her hand across
the tray of her wheelchair as if she were

using a carpenter's plane to shape
her own life from the dark.

My father, once, taught me how
to invent shapes for the smoke
he blew with his pipe, my ghosts,
he called them, before he leaned
over, breathing and swallowing them
back in. I think he understood
his own memory was becoming a ghost.

And I think that is what Adam Bennett knew,
that the nearly imperceptible blinks we make
keep us from seeing too much of the world,
and that it was right to stand
gazing towards an unknown time
as the cry of the crows
called him out beyond himself.

The Visit to an Aunt's

It takes her such a long time to descend
the stairs. And then, with the boy,
to ascend through the dull odor of boiled cabbage.
The uncle waits at the top of the stairs,
wide suspenders, wide open arms.
She tells them to mind the lace placemats,
the lace doilies that cover the arms of the chairs.

The boy lies on the floor and plays with the set
of fire engines she keeps for him. His father's
Nash Rambler has already vanished around the corner.
The legs of the furniture become houses,
the rug a field, the wall a cliff.
He is held by the way the wheels turn
as if they could go backward or forward in time.

It could be a few weeks ago, the boy
and his father visiting his father's friend.
It is dusk and he hardly notices
the early lights coming on in the barn,
the house, or the overhead light
left on in the Nash. It is so quiet
he can hear the mice in the silo.
The man and his father take a horse
to the farthest rise, stop. One of them
points the rifle and the horse falls.

Everything is so silent he believes it has not
taken place. He tries, but cannot imagine
the experience of death, the horse's, his own.
Perhaps, he wishes, we are all immortal.
A few bats flicker, testing the shadows
beneath elms. The two men are shoveling.
Everywhere there is the smell of cabbage flower. [STANZA BREAK]

58

The wheels of the fire engine keep turning
into the past, into the future. The boy knows
first the uncle, then the aunt will die.
The deaths are so close, or distant.
He turns the wheel to keep them distant.
Night descends with the boy. The Nash returns.
"You come see me," she says. But he never does.

Trying to Believe in Something

These nights since your death I imagine
you might be calling from under the sweetgum
where the swallows are darting beneath the leaves
that could pass for stars in a child's drawing,
darting to scoop the seeds released
from the round, spiked fruit the child
would draw too large on her page. All right—
there is no room left in the darkness for anything
except for the Indian pipe, those solitary
plants white and transparent as silence
you used to think the Indians made flutes of.
Once, we stayed all night in this grove,
unafraid, waiting for the swallows to reappear,
watching by the pure light of those plants.
I had thought I could believe anything.
But I have imagined the stars so cold
they might as well be ash. All I know is
the gathering sounds of swallows flecking
their wings white beneath the trees.
I am going to listen for them all night
where the Indian pipe grows in lichen,
gathering the seeds, believing again
that nothing stays lost forever.

Fox Squirrel

He is turned away, but I can see the single
yellow jacket that blurs the air around
his head, and the way the tail curls up, then flicks
carelessly as if it were part of another body.
I don't know what I must look like to him, and I
don't think he cares. It is something you might photograph,
though you'd surely miss what it is that makes him turn,
and the truth is, there may be nothing there, only
the sense that by freezing he might order a far-flung world
for a moment. The truth is, we are so often taken
by what we lose. Once in hills north of here,
where the glacier boulders told about ages I couldn't
pronounce, I followed for hours the trail of a desperate
mink who had disappeared with the quiet that time makes
on its way from one loss to another, leaving
its paw in a steel trap someone had forgotten.
This is an old story in those hills where each thing means
the loss of something else. The Shakers, who settled
there decades ago, made their precious desks
and chairs seemingly without joy. These were the people
who feared to choose, and who turned from each other,
afraid to make love and who are now nearly extinct.
I used to try to imagine them not touching, letting
the darkness fall on their long days, their flat
brooms sweeping across the barren grain floors.
Now I know that when you put out your hand
the dark is closer than you think. Too much goes on
without us not to try holding off that dark.
All around us is the luminous world the squirrel
has begun to order, the leaves beginning to turn,
revealing the large nests he has hidden all summer.
The world begins in these wishes we have for it.
The truth is, I don't think I could love you more

than now. It is only later, maybe, we will become
the part of a photograph that someone remembered wrong.
There's always a gesture or word we don't see, or hear,
showing us too late how we might have cared.
If you are sighting something then, focus the lens
where a stump or vine, or a boulder seems to blur,
making it clear, and close, and I'll be there.

Things We Could Have Been

Sometimes she talks before there is anything
to say, and when she does the small son
beside her must enter that desolate world

and anyone would take him for an orphan playing,
trying to hold on to the light that is falling
into the fields, until he notices, for all

that light, the waxwings rising, gathering,
it seems, the darkness from the previous night.
Sometimes he thinks they mean the endless

sadness his mother means. But the truth is,
she has never had a son, only this hope of one
she cannot abandon or disguise. When a friend

loses an unborn child, she thinks
it is her own son she has lost. All day
she might sit with that woman, talking

before there is anything to say, watching
the sky seem to climb away from them—
until night joins the near row of

cedar trees, disguising the way those
waxwings will take the sweet berries
and pass them down a curious line,

one to the other, passing their lives
along some branch the way those sons
might have passed a note in school. The woman [STANZA BREAK]

63

could be listening for their simple song, saying
there is nothing in the world her son couldn't be.
And now she wraps herself in that hope

and waits for her son to return. What can I
imagine to put him there? In all this dark
she needn't say what is already a part of her,

she needn't say it is only we who are left
outside, passing our own poor hopes,
more distant than a son, more orphaned than beloved.

At the Old Marblehead Burying Ground

Be still. The yellow imperial moth doesn't know
it is only late October, Indian summer, and so
he is not ready to leave the top of the headstone yet,
four stones, really, fused, cut from one rock to mark
four children who died within a month on successive years.
You can tell the worst years here, too, by how the fever
took the future from so many children—whooping cough,
someone tells us—and all the young women who died a few
days after childbirth. I don't think the moth believes
any more than we do that he is in the right place or time.
He is trying to read the plan inside him for another day.
I remember as a boy burying tin cans with messages
we'd dig up on our worst days: "Get five green apples
from MacDonough's orchard with no one seeing," or
"Mix up the clothes on the lines of five neighbors," or
the cryptic: "Find something that doesn't belong." Now
he is off, heading towards the taller, more important stones
on the top of the hill. He's nearly gone. You're right
that he tells us how much we stand to lose. One night we
                                                    held
each other so tightly we thought we had become a single
soul, and then, waking, you feared you would end your life
with no one left to hold. Be still. He is moving again,
and now I have lost the spot, though we believe he must be
going someplace we invent for him. We have buried
no messages here, but later, returning home, I will show
you how your clay pitcher whose half flower means
any field, reflects the light on its inside, showing here
and there a hint of blue, a small spot of sky that appears
and vanishes the way that moth, our love, these pasts do,
yet finding a place in the pure joy of flight and memory.

Generosity

She has come to depend upon the miraculous
generosity of whatever the wind brings,
or the easy rain that begins to tell the desert
outside the window to bloom. Outside
the window, the driftwood has turned again
into the soft desert gourds putting their roots
out into rain. She knows how the nearly
invisible amoeba, tossed for years
as if dead, come alive again in the small
arroyo basins if only they are lucky,
if only the wind was right. And so,
hearing the story of some young boy
trapped for an hour beneath a river's
ice while the men above followed
the faint shadow's drift in the currents,
before pulling him up alive where the ice
broke, it is hard for her to believe
anything could die. This is what she wants
to tell her own child, unborn, if only
they are lucky enough, who has remained
so still all this time beneath her touch.
Tonight she has remembered another small
miracle she will wait to show: the empty
sheath of a straw, compressed like an accordion
she touches with a drop of water, and it seems
to inch forward, for a moment, on the table.
And who is to say, tonight—as the rain
dissolves into itself, as the cicadas begin
again who could have been buried years
ago before emerging, climbing these trees
to sing, lucky to be alive—who is to say
that her own song does not rise on the clear
branches of air, the way a child's song rises,
believing anything, if only the wind was right.

III

All things come close and harmless
first thing this morning, a new trick of light.
Let's learn that trick. If we can, it will mean
we live in this world, neighbor to goat,
neighbor to trout, and we can take comfort
in low birds that hang long enough for us
to read markings and look up names
we'll whisper to them for now on.

—Richard Hugo, ''Distances''

Web

I think he wanted to kill me,
the brown spider that had spun all night
across the doorway, but he retreated
along the tangle of silk I made with my thrashing,
clenching himself into a ball that looked
no different than the pods he suspended in storage
between the dogberry bushes and the house.
I never saw him, never heard your warning.

Once as a child I saw my father
emerge from the crawl space beneath the porch
covered with webs, dead bees, pods,
tiny black spiders that made my mother scream,
so that my father understood what it would mean
for him to die. I never really saw that, either,
only imagined, from what they told me,
that scene which took place before my own birth
as any child will do trying to connect itself
with the lives beyond its own life and moment.

That is why our everyday details become so valuable—
a silver watch, a G.I. compass, old maps,
the wood burning of a farm, a simple touch repeated
beyond the stories we have found them in.
Sometimes I can see you as a girl learning to ride
the horse that is too large, letting it guide you
both from barrel to barrel, and suddenly

I cannot imagine not letting your hair
tangle gently across the backs of my fingers,
not drawing you closer, and then,
after a little while, feeling you rise above me,
lifting the sheets with your back, my palms

moving from the sides of your breasts to your hips,
I cannot imagine not holding you closer than our pasts,
not loving you this way forever, or to think
you would not be there at all, one or both of us
caught in the invisible webbing of a moment we never saw.

Whatever We See

When, this evening, we turned away,
you wanted to put the sky in a jar—
a handful of fireflies, taking, in one night,
what slowly changing shapes the constellations
have assumed since their dark beginnings.
I think you felt a loneliness so sudden
you needed to hold everything, even
the distance of galaxies, in your hands.
You must have risen a dozen times before
dawn to admire the moon, the way
its light dissolves our window frame,
bringing close everything we had seen today
that tells us how to begin again:
the peach orchard on the next ridge,
the resurrection fern whose brown leaves
you said would uncurl into green when wet,
the rusted river barges pushing
away from the wharves, tonight pushing
the water fog the way the leaves shifted
under our feet, and that old man selling pretzels
by the shore, his jacket and trousers stuffed
with newspapers, stuffed, he said, with half
the world. He could have been one of your Russian
dolls you open to discover smaller
copies, exact, within, as if to remind us
how we include everything within us,
how when we look inside nothing is ever lost.
I think we need to find our smallest selves
the way the clothes moth, facing
a hunger it can't satisfy, will molt into
smaller versions of itself until,
surprised by its own smallness, it becomes
desire itself. Now I see your fireflies

vanishing, turning to tiny milk stains
on the glass, and the moonlight
tightening its cocoon around you.

Today a Few Years from Now

There will always be the same man we saw selling winter
coats to the Salvation Army and buying back bright summer
jackets, mismatched, yellowed at the edges, smelling
of mothballs, smelling of new hope, the nights not spent
sleeping over the grates of the Lovemans' store exhaust.
There will always be the talk about poems, this morning
about Edmund Blunden, all his green details trying
to cover over the trenches of his past—ours and death's,
he called them—the gassed bodies stuck in poses that asked
questions too bizarre to answer, the bloated mules lining
the paths where the supply trains were shelled. I don't see
how he kept, as he said he would, the mind from drooping.
I am looking now at the flyer that has come in the bulk mail
to announce the "Revelation Lectures," Biblical prophecy,
a vision of terror that Blunden so feared. I am looking
at the white moon against the blue sky and I remember
how long it has been since I noticed that. There will always
                                                         be
that moon, Blunden's green poems, the way you keep close
the flat truth of our shadows which is also Blunden's way to
                                                       find
in any darkness, a self to forgive. There will always be this
stupid horned lark caught, as I write to you, on the porch,
flying against the screen like a moth, its mate flying against
the other side, until I poke a hole in the screen for its escape.
In the background it is Robert Schumann, a cello concerto,
Schumann, who wrote so joyfully to escape the bleak
and failing porch of his own mind, who practiced for hours
tying one finger in a sling to improve his reach, but who
crippled all hopes of playing his own music, who tried to find
places where there was so little to hear he might desire
again to write. For him, the past could be the silence we feel
with whatever songs, whatever memories we hold or invent.

That is why I must tell you that this moment goes back
to where I found as a boy a lark caught in the rusted
springs of an abandoned Buick, remembered, even then,
the earlier car on my way home from little league
practice, the whole car rocking with the two inside it
as if something invisible drove it along the road to the park.
There will always be that boy's wonder to feel what it meant
for the girl to cry, as surely as that lark, afterwards.
I wanted to climb into the back seat, to hold the girl beneath
                                        me,
the car moving towards whatever worlds I could dream.
There will always be a moment like that arriving, some face
that means the shining love of loss, that means the first
                                        awkward
shifting of lovers, and the wonder, as if it were from a life
someone else had lived, as if, in the face of some fear or hope
we could split apart as Plato says we did once before,
or become like the sea cucumber you described once:
facing a mortal danger it splits itself in two, one half to die,
one half to live. I think this is what poor Blunden meant by
                                        the second
night behind the first. I think this is what Schumann knew
when he became the several characters he hid behind to
                                        write,
when he believed the great composers dictated his music.
I think this is what my father meant when he confessed
another life, years earlier, to explain the Buick. I hardly
understood, could only watch his embarrassed face across
the fire, his trying to say a few words disguised as talk
about the night, about the river and the few fish jumping,
the names of stars, baseball, things that meant, finally,
that you don't hurt anyone, you don't forget the girl in the
                                        Buick,
the man sleeping across the grates, whomever you hurt
by intention or neglect. I am remembering all this today.
I am holding the newspaper telling the death of Norm Cash,
my father's hero, who led the league at .361. I am wishing

I could share that loss with him, or at least lean over some
wilderness fire to say how much of his life is hidden
in my own. There will always be this Schumann playing,
and for a few minutes I can imagine myself as he did,
fearing there would be no more songs, or only our lark's
muted song, so he walks into the Rhine, is pulled out later
by fishermen before committing himself to the asylum
at Edenrich. There was the smell of fish, the slick banks
of the river, the blankets they threw across him like netting.
And there would be for him two more years trying to figure
                                                        out
the coded messages he had once spelled out in his musical
notes, the way we try to find one thing in another, what
the bird on the porch or the bird in the Buick will tell us,
the way Blunden tried to escape the terror of his own past,
discovering, finally, that every life is our own life, the way
the faint whistle of the lark becomes part of Schumann's
concerto, the song which means nothing or means everything
it touches, as Schumann must have figured out that last day,
the porcelain bowl beside his table reflecting what little
light was left, the blue flowers on its sides reminding him
of distant fields, of the way his wife played the songs he
                                                        couldn't,
unable to find anything that day might mean in the years
                                                        ahead,
a day as ordinary as this, filled with failed hopes and songs,
a day ending while the notes meant only themselves, July 29,
                                                        1859.

Someone Is Always Saying Something

Even if you were here, you wouldn't spend
the last few minutes as I have peering
into the flower of the delicate pitcher plant
that has bloomed in the shadow of a cannon.
Just west of here, someone would tell you,
the Confederate lines faltered, and no one
turned back. Time was the stone someone kicked up
under his feet. But this pitcher plant—I have
been watching how, filled with water, it curls,
dissolving a spider. He must have
entered the space between two dark moments
where we peer into the history that always fails.
Sometimes we walk so deeply into that past
someone begins to remember us. That's when we think
that desire is the backward journey into ourselves.
I can't tell. But I know that entering that past
I enter you again, hearing, in the abandoned air,
someone calling my name, as if I were
leaving a place I never lived, as if the light
were rescuing a little truth from the shadows.

All There Is

I should have warned you
that the mockingbird attacks whatever crosses
its space, even you, returning after so long.
One night I watched a mockingbird
attack its own moonlight reflection
in a car window until it crushed itself.
All it knew was that window into itself.

Another night I found an old man
who'd taken an abandoned car as home,
who only wanted a window out of the dark,
and yet, I had nothing to answer his voice
the wind seemed to have carried forever,
not even the time to listen to his story.

Tonight, in the shame of my own
small love, I had been thinking
how lonely that mockingbird is
who imitates everything he can
at 2:00 A.M. in hopes of an answer.
His wings must be heavy with moonlight
and love the distances they could touch.

I had begun to believe how simple it is
that, when you take me in as surely as breath,
when, as we come together,
we save a part of each other,
that the dark is a window to ourselves,
and it no longer matters that there is
no wind so far that when we speak
our voice goes on forever.

Never Another Country

Whenever I remember how you spoke I see
the mist drifting from woods to the mountain
meadow, and I think that I am already there,
that it would be morning because the sun has risen,
though the insects are too wet to move in the grass,
beginning to dry with the sun, to vibrate.
If only you were the white-tailed doe
who stands quietly at the edge of the woods.
Can she hear what I say, or the small revelations
the owl makes folding one wing over its face?
What made me think I could stay here?
One afternoon, when you turned away, it was
as if a fire had been struck in the forest
too deep yet to be noticed, but enough
to send the meadow voles to flight.
It is a forest that is mostly pine and oak
scattered with rock falls for the fox
and muskrat, but now it will not be
the refuge I imagined we entered, where the deer
sometimes lift their heads then disappear
beneath the grassline as we approach,
because the forest is empty, dispersed,
there are no footprints left in the ash.
Our love has failed to reach so many things
that when the doe finally turns, when the white
tips of mockingbirds blink into darkness,
I fear there will be no need to wonder
at the moon's invisible half, or at such
imagined countries I try to call our own.

How We Make Sense of Things

for Chuck Scott

On some level, everything in the universe is connected.
                                    —Bell's theorem in physics

Let's say you are standing at the window, the ground mist
whitewashing the angular fences along the edges of
the river you can hardly see. There is a story—
the blind girl, how she disappeared from this house—

that keeps trying to take shape, the way
small clouds of gnats just beyond the glass collect,
disperse, or the way light surfaces briefly in the wake
of the skiff where now someone is leaning over one

end, the other end raised gently out of water.
The bottom of the river is grass, and his line is caught.
Too deep, he thinks. You look up. Depth is
what we have forgotten about the stars when we call them

heroes, utensils, animals, pretending their two dimensions
are pasted to the sky. If any of this is true, you think,
then your words become the smooth surface of the glass,
or the river. The raised end of the skiff touches down.

Let's say you are not at the window, but the blind girl is,
and when she touches the cold glass she knows
how far anything really is from what she thinks.
Sometimes she asks how deep the wind is, or sky.

Sometimes one or the other answers. Let's say she is
thinking of you as you have begun, now, to dream

of her. This is not as impossible as you think because,
as you have read somewhere, on some level everything

is connected. Let's say you are standing there after all.
Let's say it is her name you have written on the glass
you have fogged with your breath, giving everything depth,
giving her name to a world she'll never see.

Meditation for a New Moon

She is afraid, as darkness fails,
not of what the wet paths pressed
through marsh grass by some gray fox
will lead to, not even that her discovery,
earlier, of the swan's brood will recall
her own losses, but that the light is a reason

beyond her intention, the way it falls
this early across any lovers where maybe
the woman has raised her head first,
tensed, as if she heard something
the woods whisper beyond her window.
She thinks it could be the owl whose distances

brush the air that reaches her, or the moon
that depends on her for its light. She is tired
because the dark sounds fill her eyes
whether or not she chooses. She doesn't know
whether she fears what is there, or that there is
nothing. But now she begins to whisper

randomly, talking so she cannot hear
any longer, asleep so she cannot touch
the man she fears has left, her eyes
shut so she cannot see the first phrase of light,
the way it says the darkness is the darkness
in the branches that are shadowed across his face.

Storying

Even in the early group picture
he is almost cropped out, the man
who deserted the Russian Army to live
four decades in a pig shed
hidden by his wife until her death.
When he emerged, starving, believing
he might have gone on forever
undiscovered, the townspeople
shunned him, making him invisible.
The night you left I read about this,
and remembered our looking at those photos
of the west—ledges, aspen, granite
mountains, clouds—pictures so vastly
empty of people we had to invent
ourselves there to see what the camera
couldn't show, just as that deserter
placed himself at last in the world
beyond him. Sometimes we imagined
a big-eared bat hovering like a butterfly,
disguised to pluck the early moths.
Or the Indians who left their flint
chips along the ridges. Or the loud
migrations of gray squirrels we hardly
see because they never touch ground.
Their tails become umbrellas, blankets,
rudders, parachutes—whatever shape
they will need. "Storying pictures,"
we called it, in response to those
delicate eighteenth-century travelers
to the Alps who would blindfold themselves
as a protection against the fissures, crags,
the slides that offended their general sense
of the world's symmetries. I don't know how

they could live in a world they refused to see,
and I don't know what else to write you
beyond these few stories and the landscapes
I have tried to enter. First light
stirs the hornets covering their tiny
pendant nest that hangs between two
window panes. Earlier this spring
we must have missed the lone female
chewing the wooden frame to make
gray pulp. They think they'll hide
by building so obviously in the open.
I think I am going to learn the trick of
the Indians who once lived here, who could
walk among herds of deer, proving
that by putting on the poor trees, hides
and dirt of the earth they were at last
ready to live in a world where everything
important is invisible, where the self is
what we leave out of everything we love.

The Secret

It is one thing to try to tell the truth in poems.
Another to believe you have actually done it.
We talked about this one night, examining
one of those pictures where you must decipher
the things wrongly drawn: the swing hanging
by one rope to a branch, the other rope ending
halfway up, the child perfectly dressed but faceless,
the paths that end abruptly, the owl with no
wings, fish walking on the muddy shore.
So much of what we see is wrong. Tonight,
for instance, the stars reflected on the pond's
surface are not stars but the blighted leaves of an elm.
And the man, sitting with a fiberglass rod,
his float drifting like a planet among the stars
that are undisturbed except for a few casts, must have
reached into some past as out of place as anything
in that picture. Whatever way you look, something is
leaving. That, love, is the secret that we cannot name.
One night, the closer I held you, the more you seemed
to vanish, afraid, you said, that we become so much
a part of a place or a person that we seem to disappear.
A friend I know said it: every choice is somehow
also a loss. If the world were not so separate
we would not need to point out as much as we can,
swing, branch, owl, silo, horse,
we would not have to love everything, hoping in the end
for a simple truth—elm, star, pond, you,
me, words that are our poor love vanishing.

Out of Sight

How much they must know about disguises,
those grasshoppers flicking momentarily
into sight, waist high, at each of

our steps, before blending back into dry
meadow grass. The fact is, they know nothing
though we depend so much upon these imagined

gestures and signs. How else could we live?
How else could we have hoped to make
some insect or flower, some memory or wish,

say the love we seem frightened to admit?
It was in this kind of meadow where I knelt
as a boy to see a dozen caterpillars

clinging to a plank, each being
consumed by the larvae of some parasite,
amazed at such slow, silent pain,

where I knelt into a hidden nail at one
end of the plank, unable to scream.
I think it is because the past is what

we add to it that I can recall
several endings for that story. Back home
my father, searching for a lesson, might say

the ribbons tied to the fan on top of
the ice chest were a reminder for how
things we can't do without, like air, are   [STANZA BREAK]

known by what they point to, as those tadpoles,
"polywogs," we called them, kept in
jars whose lids we punched nail

holes into, waiting for frogs to appear.
I do not know what world he invented
when he learned what disease would end his dreaming

though I think he knew that anywhere a hole
into another time can appear, and we halt,
afraid, as if our minds were someplace

else—the way we felt this morning
frozen before the open mouth of
a blue jay trying to swallow

the whole sky beyond his broken wing.
Maybe what these grasshoppers say is
how we try to live in only a single

world, no better at it than the hens
and cocks fooled by yesterday's eclipse.
What we become, eventually, is afraid

of what we can't know: that man in *Time*
holding, beneath high tension wires,
a neon bulb, lit by an invisible

source, or our own exaggerated fear
that these grasshoppers are locusts swarming.
Think of the fear you showed this morning

reading about the unseen twin sun,
which they've named "Nemesis," circling ours,
due in several million years to arrive   [STANZA BREAK]

and make extinct most things that live.
Think of the end my father feared:
mouthing syllables that have no meaning,

or meanings only his dying brain would know.
Really, there are never meaningless words
as long as we listen. Do you remember

when we listened to the frightened alarm of hawks
whistling above the cliffs, and you knew then
it was a song of love? Maybe it is love

that brings us here, maybe fear,
two names we have for the same thing.
You said earlier, our minds are most kind

trying to remember what doesn't hurt,
trying to disguise, as Freud said,
the painful by our slightest details—ribbons

caterpillars, tadpoles, grasshoppers—
something exactly seen which holds us,
some small kindness we want to add.

Let me tell you then, how this morning
guided to this spot by the wood turtle
that still clings to the chain link

fence like a planet, or your fearful star,
I stumbled across the den some stray
coon hound camouflaged, crushed

unknowingly a pup she had born and licked
the placenta from already. Birthing another,
she could only shake half in horror,   [STANZA BREAK]

half in the stricken love she must have
felt. Let's believe the others she hid are
everything this meadow disguises. It is

only later we will want to name this feeling
that will seem to have taken place elsewhere
far from ourselves, or what we remember, and fear.

All the Time We Have

And when I rise from you, when the darkness I have
held begins to drift, black branch on the water,
and early carp are arching their backs to the surface.

Or when a shred of wind settles on your breast,
or when we are puzzled by the last few fireflies,
by how many things they fail to reach. Whenever,

those times, I hold your hand to my face, I can hear,
far back, a place neither of us can remember. Who is it
that is waiting for you there? The boy I knew once

who would put his ear to the rail and gauge
how soon the slow freight would come to take us
to Reading or Stoneham? All the time we had was

held by what he would say next. Also: the old man
he will become, sitting on a porch, watching the breeze
push the loose screen in and out as carelessly as gills.

Also: whoever is waiting for me. She has not forgotten
how we uncovered a hound and her half-dozen pups
sucking so hard I held my own breast in pain.

Wherever we go, someone is waiting. Whenever we love,
we enter those far places of our lives, the way
those carp nudge against a bank and disappear,

the way these words mean nothing except for you,
for the way your hand, opening with the first light,
lowers me back into this whisper of you.

What Time There Is

Sometimes I think the soul is dissolving
and not this reflection of the least moon

pushing its way across a green pond.
It is green where the algae has taken hold,

where for centuries the locust leaves,
the moss, the lichen, have filled this hole

driving the fish, even the mayflies to
abandon it, and where I can hope for no other

color this night that would replace the darkness
of your leaving and of whatever space is between us.

Nor can that deer hope, on the other shore,
its black nostrils straining, the deerflies

singing between its antlers, for he will
not touch these waters, nor will I, only

turn at the failure of light to keep
our shadows from slipping beneath the surface.

The moon will take half the night to cross
here. I remember the Cherokee legend

that the shavings from each night's diminishing
are held until each spring to flower these

locust trees; also, how each month
the sliver of fish that is left arcs,   [STANZA BREAK]

90

filling the abandoned air with its strain
to fly, filling the empty pond,

as if it had begun to discover distance,
the spaces within us, to know with the shy

lover in her beautiful thought of hesitation,
with the dying father about to hold that last

good thought in his breath, the impossibly
long flight of the soul in so brief a moment.

What to Listen For

Who listens when we talk? This is a question
Pascal asked, and answered only with the safe
bet that someone must, and the question I asked
when I went through the rain this morning to study
the museum photographs of Nazca ground drawings
taken from a plane over Peru. Etched from the dry
pampa, these enormous caterpillars, whales, foxes,
turtles, and the animals and insects no one has seen
before, were meant to evoke some response from the gods.
Which explains why they have been so carefully revised.
Which explains, too, why they were never finished.
It is still raining. How long has he been singing,
that yellow-billed cuckoo, while I have been thinking,
again, of what you said. The farmers call it a *rain crow*
because it signals approaching storms, and because
it continues, as now, arguing against the way
the rain strips the October trees. It must be calling
from the abandoned orchard, its rapid song slowing
down at the end of each burst, as if to say how it
understands the way any love is also the beginning of loss.
Once as a boy I listened as my father explained
that the snapping turtle covered with leeches we saw
slip off the bank hadn't long to live. I hardly
heard him, could only imagine the pain I thought
it felt trying to evade the slow passage
of one life into another, and felt, too, my own
life pass over into the pond. I hardly heard him.
But I think he knew, talking only to let me know
he was there. I don't think the rain crow will stop.
I think he wants to say how easy all this is,
and not enough. Today I thought you almost wept
to describe the way it seems we had drifted apart.
Nothing is ever finished. Let's take Pascal's

faith that someone is always listening, let's know
distance as something we begin to understand each time
we extend an arm in love or consolation. I could be
saying anything to you now, because I only want
to let you know I am here, that I am arguing
against the beginning of loss, against whatever silence
threatens us, using the song of this elusive bird
to say what it would mean if you went away.

The Map

It shouldn't even be here
that Leach's storm petrel which rarely
comes to shore, and seldom to this rocky
coast of Cape Ann that my tourist map
marks by a trawler larger than a town.
What the map shows are legends:
crossed picks for a quarry long closed,
a lighthouse destroyed years ago, a man
in a fisherman's slicker. And you'll find no trawlers
here, only the tiny boats of the Gloucester
tuna fleet. But that storm petrel—
it must be returning this evening
to breed among the rocks
that give, above the smell of salt and
seaweed, the musky odor of its nest.
A century ago, the Portuguese fishermen would
use the bird for a lamp by sticking
a cotton wick down its throat
to burn half the night over their charts
as if its voice were a pure beacon of light.
I imagine them wondering if the storm
that approaches too fast for escape will push
them to these reefs that have claimed
so many boats. And perhaps someone on
the lobster boat whose running lights bob
now like the flight of the petrel,
watches, as I have, the moon suddenly
take form, flame red, above the horizon
where it has been, invisible, for half an hour,
watches this solitary shape on the rocks
where the false fires of pirates
once lured ships, and hears the annoyed
bird's cry that I shouldn't be here,

at least not without the love of a woman,
you, to whom I send this message
signaling where I am, how I can be found.

A Sense of Direction

Beyond this fire and the beach, the world stutters
to name itself, never saying the same thing,
never letting you know where it begins or ends.
I can hear the drumming sound of a trawler
entering or leaving the harbor. The lighthouse,
too far to see, is trying to show me how
deep the night is. Sometimes I am afraid to guess
what happens just out of sight, as children are afraid
of places they've never been. Which way do you go?
Which way do you go when the news comes that a friend
who loses a lung to the cancer he beats
dies pointlessly when the other lung collapses?—
One night we sat on this beach trying to see
if the stars really were moving away from us.
Today, I must have watched the pelicans for hours,
their cumbersome flight showing which way the fish run.
I am sure that the trawler is heading out, after all.
And when the moon rises, there are all those other
times, and the far lights inside of things—
the shack at the end of the pier with the harbor
master asleep, the fishing boats where the crews are
about to wake, a few other campfires inside
this conch of darkness. Which way do I go?
In the morning the gulls will line up on the pier,
facing the same way. That's the way to go.